her favorite color
was yellow

poetry by
edgar holmes

1

CHAPTERS

dedicated to my loving wife

without you,
my pen would run dry
and i
would be nothing.

may her love touch you
through these pages
as it has touched me
through my life

-edgar holmes

Chapter One

Yellow

the moment i met her
my soul begged of me
to make her mine

it was as if
in the moment
i looked at her
i discovered
my life's purpose

and that
is how i fell for her

most of our lives
are spent
convincing our minds
of what the heart
already knows

when i first looked
into her eyes
i felt like i was
looking into the eyes
of someone
i had somehow
just now met
for the first time
and had yet
somehow also known
for my whole my life

freedom.

that's what her spirit
seemed to whisper
under her mask

freedom.

i can teach you
to be free.

i feel as if
i can tell you things
i would never tell
anyone else

you and i
are two souls
on the same

f r e q u e n c y

people don't tell you
who they are
up front

you have to find out
digging deep
before they reveal
their truest nature

this is the process
of making true friends
or deadly enemies

i decided to write down
everything i felt
about you

the highs and lows
the melodic complexity
of it all

i wrote it all down
sealed it into a letter
and burned it.

there is a power
between
the two of us

an electricity
we could power a city with
if only we knew how

there is something
between us
you and i

some kind
of magic

do you feel that?

the cackling energy
in the space
between our fingertips

as if the universe
is begging
for us to touch

looking back on things

i should have
declared my love for you
the moment i met you

if only
to have a few more weeks
together

my heart
my life
my soul
my everything

you.

my love for you
is etched by fire
and seared with pain
into my heart

i will never let you go
oh sweet love of mine

broken dreams
broken bottles
falling back in love
with memories of you

broken.

we either enter
or leave
this world
as such

this is our lot
as human beings
destined to live
with knowledge of pain.

when i was younger
i believed
i could reach
for the stars

now that i'm older
my feet
have remained
planted on this earth

and i, tearfully
holding my head
in my hands
wondering
if things
could've been

d i f f e r e n t . . .

the night i met her
i prayed to god;
i got on my knees
at my bedside
and i prayed
like never before

"if you just give me her
i'll give up
everything else;

wealth, fame, popularity

anything.

anything, anything for her."

and i'm so glad
that i did.

we are not born
to just

eat
work
sleep
fuck

and

die.

tell me your deepest secrets

yes, the ones
you don't even think about
to yourself
in fear that they might
somehow slip out
of your brain

tell me everything
i want to know
the
f i n g e r p r i n t s
of your soul

i swear, darling
the night we got together
the stars rejoiced
and angels danced

looking back, it's hard to
remember
just how badly life sucked
before i had her

the loneliness
the anxiety
the insecurity

how did i live
without her?

i saw her dancing
with another man
and i swear
i nearly died inside

i vowed to earn her love
and make her mine
and dance with her
throughout eternity

i want to tell you
all the small details
of my day
and listen
as you tell me
about yours

i want to be intimate
with you
verbally
spiritually
physically

i want
to be as much yours
as you are mine
so help me god.

as i walk this street alone
in the darkest of nights
in the midst of winter
watching the flickering
of streetlamps

i can't help but wish
you were with me
so i could share
even the dullest of moments
with you

in our darkest hours
brooding upon our fates
we finally understand
what we want
and who we are

x

Chapter Two

Roses

nothing makes me feel
quite so alive
as her.

the campfire
burned
brightly

we looked
up
at the stars

and i swear
i saw our paths
collide
in the cosmos

emotions fade
but feelings don't

and i feel
just as in love
with you now

as i did
the moment i knew
i loved you

if you loved me forever
everything would be okay

you
me

you always did look so good
on top

lust isn't love
but lust
is just one
of the many ways
by which i love you

somehow
you were always able
to kiss anything better

even
a broken heart

i caught feelings for you
    before i truly knew
what those feelings meant

you've got to get comfortable
with the void.

the void that appears before
you
in the midst of important
decisions

the void where infinite
possibility and infinite
brokenness live together.

gaze into it and see yourself.

woman, you make me feel
so goddamn lucky.

"bury me with roses,"
she said to me,
"bury me with seeds
so that even my death
may make the world
a little more
beautiful."

i almost wish
i had a narrator
of my life
who would expose
my inner thoughts
and feelings
and make them known

perhaps then you would known
there is not a shred of
untruth
when i tell you
i love you

she must have found
the fountain of youth
and surely
she drinks from it
every day

if i do nothing else
in this life
but tell you
how beautiful you are

i will consider it
worth it.

you are
everything good
about me

perhaps i care too much
and that has caused me
a tremendous amount of pain
during my life

but in you i found someone
who saw how much i cared
and appreciated it
and even returned it tenfold

and so i consider the pain
more than worth it.

i promise you
as long as i'm alive
you will have flowers
on your dresser
and shoulder rubs
when you're stressed

as long as i'm alive
i promise you
i will love you
with everything i am.

it would take me
an eternity
to tell you
all the ways
i love you..

but let me try.

there is something
so beautiful
about the way
our hands
intertwine.

i will make you happy
and die trying

for i will never
take you for granted.

i don't care
if i get to have
all the things
i always dreamed
of having

all i really care about
is having you.

the dance of romance
went on and on
and we danced with other
people

i couldn't help
but look at you
and know
that when i got the chance
i would ask you to dance
and i would make you
never want to stop.

i don't want to escape life
as long as you're in it

why would i waste a second
i could've spent with you?

x

Chapter Three

Meadows

i am endlessly fascinated
by the way it felt
before you were mine
the sheer need
i had never felt before

we were smoking in your car
just friends at the time

we were just talking
about why it feels so good
to kiss another person

-it's such an odd act
the pressing together
of lips
if you think about it-

we were talking about kissing
and i couldn't help
but lean over
and kiss you

she was always
a better artist
than me

she seemed to pull
imaginative ideas
out of nowhere
and draw
from an endless fountain
i could only dream of

and yet she looks lovingly
upon what i create
giving me encouragement

i long to be broken by you
in ways no one else has

i would adore the scars you
gave me
knowing it meant
i got to be touched
by you

no matter the distance
life puts between us
i know we will always
find our ways back
to each other.

saying goodbye
to you
is a happy thing

because i get to say
hello
all over again
tomorrow

there is nothing
that can quite describe
the agony
of not being yours

so this is what it feels like
to finally meet someone
who exists
on the same frequency
as you do

there's a harmony to it
a blissful feeling
that we belong together

i want to give you
everything

including
my last name

is it really such a bad thing
that two broken people
should find each other
in the dark of night
and make their own light
together?

you are my sun, moon, and
stars

blue. cold. sharp.

the world without you.

in those few days
where we broke up
i realized just how cruel
the world can be
and how cruel you must become
to cope with it

my mind is filled with things
i could never express. most of
them are about you. perhaps i
think about you more than i
should. perhaps i am just a
sick man, fixated on the idea
of a love that can never be.
but i will never stop trying.

not until it kills me.

love is happiness and poison.

my darling,

i've been looking for you
since i drew my first breath

the imprint of your soul
on mine
was something i knew i needed
since the very beginning

before you, life was like
holding my breath

and you were the oxygen i
needed

i never felt
like i was

e n o u g h

for anyone
or anything
until   i met
you

she is so much more
passionate
about things
than i could ever be

the way she talks about
her views on life
and existence
make me fall even further
in love
with who she is.

"you talk about me like i'm
some kind of goddess. and
maybe you see me that way
sometimes.

but remember that i am flawed,
i'm just a human being, and i
don't belong on a pedestal.

let them know about my flaws,
let them know the ways i've
hurt you, let them know that i
was never perfect. because
that's what love is.
imperfect.

love is two people accepting
each others' imperfections and
making it work no matter what.

 that's the kind of love we
have- something real,
something true, something
human. "

you broke every rule for me

when i lose my memory
as i get older
i don't think i'll remember
the grand romantic gestures

i think i'll remember
grocery shopping together
watching tv in our pajamas
the way you made me feel
as if i never had to be alone

when i forget everything else
in life
i will never forget
the way it felt
to be yours.

a string quartet
could not articulate
what i feel
for you

she didn't like being
labelled.

she didn't like being
categorized
put in boxes
or told who she was

she was her own person
who defied expectations
and was always
one step ahead
of what everyone thought of
her

through the darkest night
as long as i have
you by my side
i will always have
enough

x

Chapter Four

Sunlight

fall in love with someone
who you want to be
more like

she was a mystery

at once unknowable
and intimate

there could never be
anyone like
her.

if you only love her
for what she does for you

you don't really love her.

the only way
to cheat death
is to adapt
to life.

love is like karma

you get what you give

if you remember
to be grateful
for the good in your life

no one
can truly
hurt you.

question everything
you're told.

i wish you could see
the universes
i see
behind your eyes

i wish you could see
how truly beautiful
you are
to me

if i could stay
in this very moment
with you
forever

i would.

the art of listening
is underrated

too often we only think
of what we're going to say

and not really
what the other person is
saying

you are my ray of sunshine

there is no mountain
we cannot climb
together

there is no river
too swift
for us to cross

there is nothing
our love
cannot
overcome

most of our lives
are spent
reaching out
into the darkness
searching for
answers
that aren't there.

all i want
is you

our love is one
forged by fire
and molded by experience

together
we are something
beautiful

you and i
were meant
to be
together

my definition
of perfection
is you

if i ever love
someone else
i know
that it could only be
a cheap charade
an imitation
of what i had
with you

please, god

if nothing else
in this life
let me love her
till the day i die

she's the type of woman
who knows 'normal'
isn't a compliment

i love you
not just to stop
the feeling
of being alone

but because
i'm only my best self
when i'm with you.

every morning
as i wake up
next to you

i thank my lucky stars
that i get to live out
what i used to imagine
as my perfect life

as long as i have you
i am complete.

110

thank you for reading my debut
collection of poetry.

thank you for giving my words
a chance and letting me speak
my mind.

i am eternally grateful to
those who support my creative
endeavors; having to work a 9-
to-5 job again would be the
death of me.

blessings to you and yours,
and may you be lucky enough to
find a love like i have.

-edgar holmes

Printed in Poland
by Amazon Fulfillment
Poland Sp. z o.o., Wrocław